Amish in Michigan

DISCOVERING THE PEOPLES OF MICHIGAN
Arthur W. Helweg and Linwood H. Cousins, Series Editors

Ethnicity in Michigan: Issues and People
Jack Glazier, Arthur W. Helweg

French Canadians in Michigan
John P. DuLong

African Americans in Michigan
Lewis Walker, Benjamin C. Wilson, Linwood H. Cousins

Albanians in Michigan
Frances Trix

Jews in Michigan
Judith Levin Cantor

Amish in Michigan
Gertrude Enders Huntington

Italians in Michigan
Russell M. Magnaghi

Discovering the Peoples of Michigan is a series of publications examining the state's rich multicultural heritage. The series makes available an interesting, affordable, and varied collection of books that enables students and lay readers to explore Michigan's ethnic dynamics. A knowledge of the state's rapidly changing multicultural history has far-reaching implications for human relations, education, public policy, and planning. We believe that Discovering the Peoples of Michigan will enhance understanding of the unique contributions that diverse and often unrecognized communities have made to Michigan's history and culture.

Amish in Michigan

Gertrude Enders Huntington

Michigan State University Press

East Lansing

⊚ The paper used in this publication meets the minimum requirements
of ANSI/NISO Z39.48-1992 (R 1997) (Permanence of Paper)

Michigan State University Press
East Lansing, Michigan 48823-5202
Printed and bound in the United States of America

07 06 05 04 03 02 01   1 2 3 4 5 6 7

LIBRARY OF CONGRESS CATALOGING-IN-PUBLICATION DATA
Huntington, Gertrude Enders.
Amish in Michigan / Gertrude Enders Huntington.
p. cm. — (Discovering the peoples of Michigan)
Includes bibliographical references and index.
ISBN 0-87013-597-X (alk. paper)
1. Amish—Michigan—History. 2. Amish—Michigan—Social conditions.
3. Amish—Michigan—Social life and customs. 4. Michigan—Ethnic
relations. 5. Michigan—History. I. Title. II. Series.
F575.M45 H86 2001
977.4'0088287—dc21
2001002538

Discovering the Peoples of Michigan. The editors wish
to thank the Kellogg Foundation for their generous support.

Cover design by Ariana Grabec-Dingman
Book design by Sharp Des!gns, Inc.

COVER PHOTO: Amish Buggy with slow-moving vehicle symbol.
Cover and all uncredited photos are by G. E. Huntington

Visit Michigan State University Press on the World Wide Web at:
www.msupress.msu.edu

To the memory of David C. Huntington,
art historian, and to our children
Abigail, Daniel, and Caleb.

SERIES ACKNOWLEDGMENTS

Discovering the Peoples of Michigan is a series of publications that resulted from the cooperation and effort of many individuals. The people recognized here are not a complete representation, for the list of contributors is too numerous to mention. However, credit must be given to Jeffrey Bonevich, who worked tirelessly with me on contacting people as well as researching and organizing material.

The initial idea for this project came from Mary Erwin, but I must thank Fred Bohm, director of the Michigan State University Press, for seeing the need for this project, for giving it his strong support, and for making publication possible. Also, the tireless efforts of Keith Widder and Elizabeth Demers, senior editors at Michigan State University Press were vital in bringing DPOM to fruition. Keith put his heart and soul into this series, and his dedication was instrumental in its success.

Otto Feinstein and Germaine Strobel of the Michigan Ethnic Heritage Studies Center patiently and willingly provided names for contributors and constantly gave this project their tireless support.

My late wife, Usha Mehta Helweg, was the initial editor. She meticulously went over manuscripts. Her suggestions and advice were crucial. Initial typing, editing, and formatting were also done by Majda Seuss, Priya Helweg, and Carol Nickolai.

Many of the maps in the series were drawn by Fritz Seegers while the graphics showing ethnic residential patterns in Michigan were done by the Geographical Information Center (GIS) at Western Michigan University under the directorship of David Dickason. Additional maps have been contributed by Ellen White.

Russell Magnaghi must also be given special recognition for his willingness to do much more than be a contributor. He provided author contacts as well as information to the series' writers. Other authors and organizations provided comments on other aspects of the work. There are many people that were interviewed by the various authors who will remain anonymous. However, they have enabled the story of their group to be told. Unfortunately, their names are not available, but we are grateful for their cooperation.

Most of all, this work is a tribute to the writers who patiently gave their time to write and share their research findings. Their contributions are noted and appreciated. To them goes most of the gratitude.

ARTHUR W. HELWEG, *Series Co-editor*

Contents

The Amish in Michigan[1]

This is the eighth summer for us to farm in Mich. We have never regretted moving into this area.[2]

Driving along the rural roads of any of twenty counties in Michigan one may suddenly come upon a black buggy driven by a bonneted woman or a bearded Amish man. Though the Amish ride in cars, they may not drive or own cars; most do not have "high-line" electricity in their buildings or telephones inside their homes. They adhere to a strict dress code and speak a German dialect known colloquially as "Pennsylvania Dutch." Originally, the Michigan Amish were part of the better known, larger Indiana Amish settlement but now there are also communities in Michigan with settlers from Ohio, Canada, Illinois, and Pennsylvania. Today the Amish, with their unique lifestyle, are found only in North America where approximately 170,000 live in twenty-four states and one Canadian province. The few European congregations that did not emigrate gradually lost their distinctive identity. Contemporary Amish represent a conscientious, growing population with three-fourths of their children choosing to join the church of their parents'. In order to better understand these American citizens we will look at their historical background, their immigration into Michigan, their occupations, marriage patterns, culture conflicts, community-financed schools, their medical practices, and their cultural survival.

Historical Background

The Amish, living on small, family-sized farms in rural Michigan, are recent immigrants to the state. In 1955 there were fewer than five hundred Amish in the state; forty years later there were about six thousand and by 2000 there were just over seven thousand. Four-fifths of these have moved to Michigan since 1975, bringing with them a tradition of improving marginal land by practicing labor-intensive, frugal farming, utilizing horse-drawn equipment and shunning the use of electricity both in the barn and in the house. Their distinctive dress (dark buttonless jackets with broad-brimmed black hats for men, long, solid-colored dresses with white head coverings and black bonnets for women) coupled with travel in horse-drawn buggies, brand the Amish as anomalies in contemporary society, eliciting both fascination and skepticism from fellow citizens.

The Amish descend from the Anabaptists, a radical sect that originated in 1525 among the Reformation followers of Zwingli in Zurich, Switzerland, when in a prayer meeting the worshipers instituted adult baptism. Beliefs that distinguish them to this day are (1) adult baptism, (2) separation of church and state, (3) nonresistance, (4) not swearing oaths, and (5) personal accountability to one another within the community of believers. In order to receive a believer's baptism, an individual must be mature enough to distinguish right from wrong, have heard the word preached, believed the message, and confessed the faith. These prerequisites negate infant baptism and reject the state's right to dictate the religious affiliation of its subjects, thus creating a separation of church and state and, *ipso facto*, freedom of religion. Refusal to swear an oath, along with nonresistance, which demanded refusal to serve in any military activity, also threatened the power of the secular government. In spite of severe persecution, the nonviolent Swiss Brethren segment of the Anabaptists attracted many converts who gradually became know as Mennonites after an early Dutch leader Menno Simons (1496-1561). Similarly, the Amish are named after Jacob Ammann, a Swiss Mennonite elder who, in 1693, precipitated a division among the Alsatian and Swiss Mennonite churches by preaching a strict church discipline and demanding avoidance of disobedient church members in all social interaction. Communion was to be held twice a year instead of only once, and foot-washing was added to the service. Hair and dress styles were determined by the church and interaction with those outside the religious fellowship was severely restricted. Amish still celebrate communion twice a year and practice foot-washing as part of the service. They will not eat or participate in social activities with a person who is under the *Bann*. Individuals under the *Bann* have been ritually removed from church membership. The Amish do not ban for wrong thoughts or heresy, only for wrong behavior. After a banned individual has illustrated repentance by everyday action and has made a formal confession in front of the members of his/her own congregation, the erring individual is then often welcomed back into the church.

A division developed among the Amish in the third quarter of the nineteenth century. Those congregations who continued to worship in their homes rather than in meeting houses, who observed strict shunning of excommunicated members, who read prayers and Scripture in high German, and who followed their local church discipline or *Ordnung* became known as Old Order Amish. The *Ordnung* represents the consensus of the community on acceptable behavior detailing aspects of dress, occupation, equipment, and various specifics of lifestyle. The *Orndung* is generally unwritten. It can be changed or modified as part of the semiannual preparation for communion. Because the Amish are strictly congregational in their church organization, differences develop among church districts that can lead to non-communing aggregates. Beginning in the 1960s some Amish congregations were referred to as New Order Amish. These districts maintain the distinctive dress and use horse and buggy transportation but they are more lenient in church discipline and in the use of technology. The Michigan Amish vary in their degree of rejection of technology from the strict Swartzentruber branch of the Old Order Amish to the more liberal New Order Amish. All the Amish who drive horse and buggies will be treated as a single socioreligious ethnic group. The contributions of the Mennonites, who are allowed to drive and own cars, will not be discussed.

The Amish were early immigrants to the New World. They came in two waves: 1727-1770 and 1815-1850. The eighteenth-century immigrants came from Switzerland and the Palatinate, landed in Philadelphia, and settled in Pennsylvania. The nineteenth-century arrivals, including the ancestors of many of today's Michigan Amish, came from Switzerland via Alsace, Lorraine, Montbeliard, Waldeck, Hesse, and Bavaria. Some landed in New Orleans and settled in Ohio, Indiana, Illinois, and Iowa; some landed in Philadelphia and New York and came to the Midwest through Pennsylvania; others landed in Baltimore and settled in Maryland, New York, and Ontario.[3] Seventy percent of the approximately 170,000 Amish lived in three states: Ohio, Pennsylvania, and Indiana. The next three states with the largest, though much smaller, Amish populations are Wisconsin, Michigan, and Missouri.

Communication among these geographically separated settlements approximates the face-to-face interaction characteristic of Amish culture. A weekly paper, *The Budget*, enables friends and families to stay in neighborly contact with one another. Over 350 "scribes," more than half of whom are Amish, submit almost weekly letters reporting events in their local communities. Seventeen scribes from Amish settlements in Michigan had letters in the 17 January 1990 *Budget;* in the 19 January 2000 issue, 33 scribes wrote from Michigan. Scribes report such events as a butter bee at which the women made two hundred pounds of butter for the cheese house; graveside services for a still-born boy who had been delivered by Caesarian section; red-tape over having a cemetery on the farm, and events such as where church was held and who has been visiting whom.

Immigration to Michigan

By Amish standards, the earliest attempts at settlement in Michigan were unsuccessful in that the members have either moved away or joined non-Amish churches.

The Amish have evolved a unique community structure essential to their survival as a discrete subculture. They must have at least one local church district in order to maintain their identity. Ideally, each church district includes a bishop, two preachers, and a deacon. For a limited period of time a community can function under the care of a non-resident bishop who comes in to help with communion, baptisms,

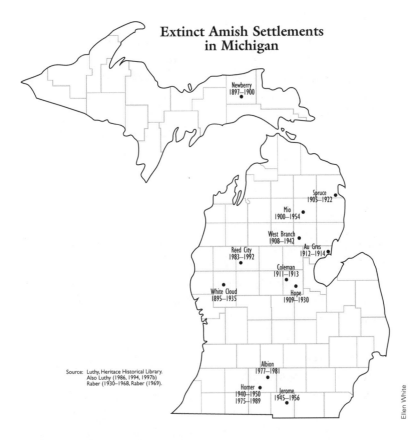

Extinct Amish Settlements in Michigan

Newberry
1897–1900

Spruce
1905–1922

Mio
1900–1954

West Branch
1908–1942

Au Gres
1912–1914

Reed City
1983–1992

Coleman
1911–1913

White Cloud
1895–1935

Hope
1909–1930

Albion
1977–1981

Homer
1940–1950
1975–1989

Jerome
1945–1956

Source: Luthy, Heritace Historical Library.
Also Luthy (1986, 1994, 1997b)
Raber (1930–1968, Raber (1969).

Ellen White

Figure 1. Map of extinct settlements

weddings, and ordinations. For an even shorter period they can rely on visiting ministers, but if no ordained clergy join the settlement, or if no resident is ordained, the settlement is doomed to fail. The individual farms that make up an Amish settlement are not necessarily contiguous but are interspersed among non-Amish neighbors. The Amish-owned farms, clustered along back roads, must be close enough for the Amish to visit one another easily. A church district should be small enough for all the families to fit into one home for the Sunday church service. Due to the communal nature of their social structure, settlements are generally started by clusters of families, who are often related. An older couple and several sons and sons-in-law, or several married brothers and sisters, may move together to a new location. Occasionally a single family will move in advance of the other. Their loneliness shows in the following plea soliciting coreligionists to join them:

> We wish some more people would come and settle here, so we could have church. We are the only Amish family living in Midland Co. Come and see the beautiful country while it is yet cheap and while you have a good choice. (1909).[4]

The first Amish families to move to Michigan came from Indiana in 1895, settling near White Cloud (Newaygo). Land was cheap, selling for between $2.50 and $5.00 an acre of logged-over land. Most of the settlers farmed; however, many of them supplemented their income by working on logging crews in the winter. Three men set up sawmills, producing lumber for needed buildings. After the pine and oak stumps were removed and the sandy loam was dressed with manure, the land produced good crops of wheat, corn, millet, hay, oats, rye, and potatoes. Larger quantities of manure were needed than the farms generated and productivity decreased with each year of cropping. Today the area where the Amish lived is part of the Manistee National Forest. Considerably less successful was an attempt to settle in the Upper Peninsula (1897). The six families from Ohio found the winters too hard and the growing season too short for farming. After only three years all had moved back to Ohio or south to the new Amish settlement near Mio (Oscoda). The Mio settlement, started in 1900 by families from Ohio, was successful financially; by 1954, however, it was no longer Amish as most of the members had joined the neighboring, more liberal Mennonites and were driving cars and farming with tractors. Beginning in 1970, a new influx of Amish from Ohio and Indiana established a community in the same area.[5] By 2000 this community was flourishing, with three church districts and approximately four hundred children and adults.

Map of One Amish Church District

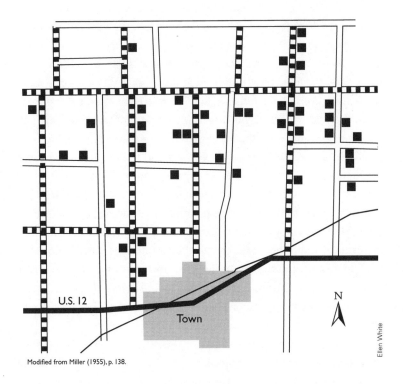

Modified from Miller (1955), p. 138.

Figure 2. Amish households located along rural roads, interspersed among English households.

In 1852 Joseph Schwartz, an eighteen-year-old Swiss Amish youth, immigrated from Montbeliard, France. He settled in Allen County Indiana where he was eventually ordained a minister and then a bishop. In 1905 Bishop Schwartz, accompanied by his son and son-in-law, migrated from Indiana to Spruce, making this Alpena County community the only Michigan Amish settlement with a European-born founder.[6] The sandy soil was stony and did not produce good crops. The men worked during the winter months cutting and hauling logs, cutting firewood, making cedar fence posts, and putting up buildings for non-Amish. One man did custom feed grinding. In spite of the supplementary work, the Amish never prospered on the poor soil. Most of the thirteen families who had settled in the area stayed fewer than five years.

West Branch (Ogemaw), Hope (Midland), Coleman (Midland), and Au Gres (Arenac) were founded between 1908 and 1912. West Branch and Hope were the most tenacious, lasting thirty-six and twenty-one years, respectively. West Branch had at least twenty-eight families, and Hope more than fifty. Most of the West Branch immigrants came originally from Ontario. Although the Michigan soil was good, the families were so closely related that marriage partners had to be sought elsewhere, preferably in Ontario. A few families moved to other Michigan Amish districts, but most returned to Canada. By contrast, the Amish who settled near Hope came from various Indiana communities and several other Midwestern states. This heterogeneous settlement was plagued by disunity and strife. Some joined the Mennonites; others moved to settlements in Indiana, Ohio, Illinois, and elsewhere in Michigan. Coleman (Midland) 1911-1913 and Au Gres (Arenac) 1912–c.1914 were small and short-lived. The few families moved on to other settlements or affiliated with the Mennonites.

Homer (Calhoun) (1940-1950) was settled primarily by Amish from two separate regions: Centerville, Michigan and Daviess County, Indiana, each with its own traditions and *Ordnung*. Two years after Homer was settled, a woman wrote to the *Budget*:

> Well we like Michigan a lot better then we expected and will tell about some of our crops.
>
> Our wheat made 275 bu. from 14 acres, and our oats made 1015 bu. from 19 acres. Our early potatoes did well too. We planted one bu. of our own seed and got 16 bushels of nice potatoes. How is that for Michigan? We were told before we came here, if we go to Michigan, we can't raise any crops.
>
> I urge each one to come and look for themselves. Everyone that has been to see us since we live here was surprised at the country we have here.
>
> People are very friendly and we really have good neighbors. (20 August 1942)[7]

Table 1: Amish Settlements in Michigan

FOUNDED	SETTLEMENT NAME	COUNTY	FOUNDED–DISBANNED
	White Cloud	Newaygo	1895–1935
	Newberry	Luce	1897–1900
	Mio	Oscoda	1900–1954
	Spruce	Alpena	1905–1922
	West Branch	Ogemaw	1908–1942
	Hope	Midland	1909–1930
1910	Centreville	St. Joseph	
	Coleman	Midland	1911–1913
	Au Gres	Arenac	1912–c.1914
	Homer	Calhoun	1940–1950
	Jerome	Hillsdale	1945–c.1956
1956	Camden	Hillsdale	
1960	California	Branch	
1970	Mio	Oscoda	
1971	Bronson	Branch	
1973	Greenville	Montcalm	
	Homer	Calhoun	1975–1989
	Albion	Calhoun	1977–1981
1977	Quincy	Branch	
1977	Charlotte	Eaton	
1978	Hale	Iosco	
1979	Gladwin (Swtr)	Gladwin	
1979	Reading	Branch/Hillsdale	
1980	Gladwin	Gladwin	
1981	Scottville/Ludington	Mason	
1981	Clare	Clare	
1981	Rosebush	Isabella	
1982	Stanwood	Mecosta	
	Reed City	Osceola	1983–1992
1983	Blanchard	Isabella	
1987	Marlette	Sanilac	
1987	Elsie/Ovid	Clinton	
1989	Homer	Calhoun	
1989	Evart	Osceola	
1990	Fremont/Holton	Newaygo	
1991	Coral	Montcalm	
1993	Cass City	Tuscola	
1993	Manton	Wexford	
1993	Vestaburg	Montcalm	
1994	Newaygo	Newaygo	
1995	Marion	Osceola	
1995	Ossineke	Alpena	
1997	Osseo	Hillsdale	
1998	Bloomingdale	Van Buren	

Some communities cross county boundaries, and in some cases the land is in one county and the post office address is in another. Location of major land holdings is used in determining the county.

Sources: Luthy, 1986, 1992, 2000; Luthy, personal communication; *1975 Michigan Directory; The Budget; 1987 Michigan Directory;* Raber, *Calender; 1995 Michigan Directory.*

In spite of the good report, this Homer community lasted only ten years. The original settlers brought with them different traditions and two *Ordnung*. Because they were unable to resolve their differences, one group started a new community near Jerome (1945–c. 1956.)[8] This community did well agriculturally but differences persisted and a rowdy element developed among the young people, who would sometimes dress in "English"[9] clothes, play baseball on Sunday afternoons, and participate in the large singings held by some of the more rebellious Indiana Amish young people. Internal problems, variation in strength of Amish convictions, and lack of agreement over the creation of an Amish school when the rural one-room school was closed, all contributed to the demise of the community. In addition to the closing of the rural school, a law requiring school attendance to the age of sixteen was enforced, resulting in Amish youth being forced to attend high school in North Adams. In 1949, the more conservative families left Michigan for Ohio and eventually moved to Ontario, where they now operate their own parochial schools with no interference from the government or pressure to send their children to school outside the community.

In 1975, another settlement was started near Homer, but church disunity caused it also to disband after about fourteen years. The farms were sold to still other Amish who in 1989 established a new church district, bringing a minister from Indiana to lead church services. By 2000 this new Homer community had opened its own schools and had ordained its own bishop, ministers, and deacons.

The first three permanent Amish settlements in Michigan (1910, 1956, 1960) were in the southern counties of St. Joseph, Hillsdale, and Branch. Functionally they were part of the large Indiana communities. After 1970, Amish settlements in Michigan increased rapidly. Between 1970 and 1975 three successful Amish settlements were started in Oscoda (Mio), Branch (Bronson), and Montcalm (Greenville) counties. By 1975 the Amish population in Michigan had increased to just over one thousand. Seven new settlements began between 1980 and 1985, bringing the population to more than 3,000. In the next five years, the addition of five settlements brought the Amish population in the state to more than 4,600. By 1995 there were twenty-nine Amish settlements,

Figure 3. Map of Amish settlements, 2000

with fifty church districts, located in twenty Michigan counties. By 2000 the Michigan Amish population had grown to approximately seven thousand.

These geographically discrete settlements are characterized by considerable visiting and mutual support among related Amish communities. A letter from Michigan in the *Budget* reports:

The buildings on Marlin Hochstetler's property are making progress . . . On Friday and Sat. he had a frolic for the community. A van load from

Table 2: Michigan Amish Growth and Estimated Population

DATE	NUMBER OF COUNTIES	NUMBER OF SETTLEMENTS	NUMBER OF CHURCH DISTRICTS	ESTIMATED POPULATION
1955	2	2	4	480
1960	3	3	5	600
1965	3	3	6	720
1970	4	4	7	840
1975	6	7	10	1,200
1980	8	13	13	1,560
1985	14	19	28	3,360
1990	16	22	39	4,680
1995	19	29	50	5,650
2000	20	31	59	7,180

Sources: Luthy, Personal Communication; Luthy, (1985, 1992,1994, 1997); Miller (1975), Miller (1987, 1995); Raber, *Calender* (1939–2000); *The Budget*.

Population estimate based on average of 20 households per district, six persons per household.

Hale were up to help. Yest. a van load from Evart and Rosebush were here to help too. He wants to have the barn finished for first crop hay.[10]

There are now so many different Amish settlements in Michigan that theoretically one could travel by horse and buggy from the Indiana border to the tip of the lower peninsula spending each night in a different Amish community.

Occupations

Although fewer and fewer Amish are full-time farmers, farming is definitely the preferred occupation. In Michigan, many Amish farm families need to supplement their income with other occupations such as crafts, selling baked goods, maple syrup, garden produce, and quilts. Of the 627 heads of households listed in the *1995 Michigan Directory*,[11] 237 list farming as their sole occupation.[12] Another 94 listed farming combined with other occupations such as carpentry, construction, lumbering or sawmilling.

There is some specialized farming among the Michigan Amish, especially dairy farming to produce milk for several cheese houses. Vegetable cooperatives and produce auctions have been established in various Amish communities, enabling their produce to be marketed more efficiently than can be done by individual families driving horse-drawn wagons. Some full time diversified farmers follow a traditional four- or five-year rotation. Corn is followed by oats, wheat, if included in the rotation, is sown after the oats are harvested, and in the spring the growing wheat is top-seeded with legume seeds. After the wheat is cut, the hay grows and is ready for several cuttings the following spring and summer; finally, it is pastured in the fall. During the winter the sod is covered with strawy manure from the barn and in the early spring the field is plowed, preparing it for corn as the cycle continues. The mixture of straw and manure lightens the soil; cultivation destroys the slugs' burrows and the weeds, which reduces the need for herbicides. The

Figure 4. Bringing in the washing. All laundry, washing, drying, and ironing is done without the benefit of electricity.

Table 3: Michigan Occupations by County

OCCUPATION*	Branch	Clare	Clinton	Eaton	Gladwin	Hillsdale	Iosco	Isabella	Mason	Montcalm	Newaygo	Osceola	Oscoda	St. Joseph	Sanilac	Tuscola	TOTAL
Farming Only	30	25	1	11	23	13	7	10	10	17	10	5	10	24	26	15	237
Farming Plus	34	6	0	4	4	2	3	2	1	5	1	0	7	16	8	1	94
Total Farming**	64	31	1	15	27	15	10	12	11	22	11	5	17	40	34	16	331
Carpentry/Construction	35	3	0	12	4	1	3	1	8	2	2	0	7	8	7	0	93
Factory Work	0	0	0	0	0	0	0	0	0	0	0	0	0	50	0	0	50
Lumber Sawmill	4	7	0	0	4	2	1	0	2	10	0	5	18	1	1	1	56
Shop	5	16	0	6	5	1	0	2	4	5	3	4	14	10	2	0	77
Furniture/Woodwork	1	3	5	2	2	0	0	2	2	3	2	1	4	3	0	1	31
DaylaborUnlisted	7	6	0	1	0	1	0	4	2	7	1	2	2	12	0	4	49
Retired	0	1	0	1	3	0	0	1	1	1	1	0	0	10	3	0	22
Miscellaneous	0	7	2	0	0	0	0	1	1	4	1	0	4	4	1	0	25
Number of Households	85	64	8	35	42	22	10	21	27	47	19	17	53	117	40	20	

Compiled from *Michigan Amish Directory 1995*. *Some households reported occupations in more than one category. **Aggregate of two preceding farming categories.

Figure 5. Amish farmstead, showing house, barn, outbuildings, windmill, bird-house, clothesline poles, steel-rimmed wagon, hitching rack. St. Joseph County, Eldon Hamm, photographer.

light, horse-drawn equipment does not compact the soil, making water penetration more efficient. Planting different crops each year reduces the need for insecticides because there are few crop-damaging insects in a field that has not been planted in the same crop for four or five years. Land can be worked earlier in the spring with light horse-drawn equipment than with heavy tractors. All Amish farms have horses and most have other livestock such as cows, hogs, and chickens, and sometime sheep, goats, and rabbits. The Amish cultivate large kitchen gardens in which they raise most of their food for the table and may grow garden produce to sell. Part time farmers may specialize in such crops as melons, cucumbers, berries, maple syrup, sheep, or steers. The community orientation of the Amish contributes to their growing interest in produce cooperatives. They have a long tradition of working together and helping each other with barn raisings, quilting, establishing cheese houses, and building their community schools.

The Amish take good care of their fields and gardens. Attention to the buildings varies, and they are less concerned with their pastures, woodlots, and wetlands. On small farms there is a tendency to overgraze pastures, woodland, and stream banks and to overcut woodlots.

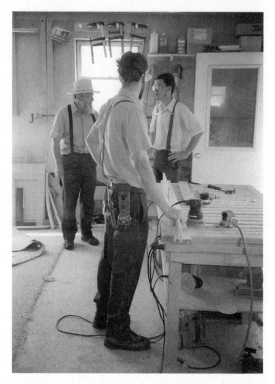

Figure 6. Cabinet Shop. In this non-electric enterprise, the tools are air-powered.

Wildlife is abundant on Amish farms because small fields in different stages of rotation provide a variety of habitats; the fence rows offer cover and undisturbed ground, and use of pesticides is minimal, causing less violence to wildlife. Amish farms often have bird houses and bird feeders. Many types of wildlife flourish where there is a variety of trees, bushes, grass and water and a mixture of woods and clearings. Wildlife is more abundant on a small Amish farm than in the neighboring state forest.

Carpentry and construction are the most common occupations after farming. When Amish purchase non-Amish farms, they modify the existing buildings to conform to the requirements of their religion. Electricity and central heating systems are removed or disconnected; in the strictest districts plumbing may be torn out. Wood stoves are installed for cooking and heating. The downstairs of the farmhouse is adapted to accommodate large numbers of people for church services, which are always held in the house or barn. (The average population of a Michigan Amish church district is between 120 and 200 although there is considerable variation.) The kitchen is enlarged as this room functions as the center of the household. Not only is it the locale for cooking and canning, but for eating meals; often there will be one or two treadle sewing machines ready for quick mending jobs. New buildings are usually needed for efficient pursuit of the generalized, diversified farming practiced by the Amish. Unlike specialized farming or agribusiness, Amish farmsteads are characterized by large barns with supplementary buildings accommodating various types of live stock. There are buildings to store corn, silage, other feed for the animals, and farm equipment. A windmill or a pump house may be erected and a spring house built; or, perhaps a milk house. Some farms have an ice house or a wash house. The small shops managed by the Amish are built on their farms. Carpentry crews offer good training for young, unmarried Amish men and they bring cash into the community by doing specific jobs for the "English." A typical distribution of occupations was reported for her settlement by one of the *Budget* scribes:

> Among us we have 11 dairies, some more farmers, carpenters, several are at home helping on dairies, 2 cabinet shops, 2 harness shops, one horse-shoer, 2 engine shops, and rest are carpenters or day laborers. One log home builder who also has an oak furniture store.[13]

In St. Joseph County on the Indiana border, fifty heads of households were listed in the *1995 Directory* as working in (non-union) factories mostly over the border in Indiana. In the rest of Michigan, no Amish man was recorded as a factory worker; non-farmers were more likely to work in a sawmill, at lumbering, or as a woodworker or painter. Amish communities need specialized shops and repair services to modify and maintain their horse-drawn implements, to stock and service the small engines that drive their non-electrical equipment, and to supply their lamps, irons, and other non-electrical appliances. Small shops operated by the Amish serve the community by making harnesses, repairing shoes, crafting buggies, and selling foods such as sugar, flour, tapioca, and needed goods such as plain colored fabrics, sewing notions, hardware, kitchen items, and books. Often these shops are owned by retired farmers or men with physical handicaps that preclude their farming. There are Amish-run bakeries, cabinet shops, and several small furniture shops that make typical Amish bent-wood hickory rockers. Amish women may have a greenhouse and small stores, and sell garden produce, baked goods, and quilts.[14] In the most traditional Amish church districts, almost all of the family heads farm.

Marriage Patterns

Within the Amish, subgroups with similar *Ordnung* (church rules) tend to intermarry. Similarities in *Ordnung* and marriage ties are more important than geographic distance and political boundaries both for visiting patterns and for a sense of unity and identification. This explains why Michigan's Hillsdale settlement is included in the *Indiana Amish Directory of Allen County and Vicinity (1970)* and why the Hillsdale churches were omitted from the 1975 and 1987 *Michigan Directories.* The Quincy, Michigan settlement was included in the Indiana *Amish Directory: Allen County, South Whitley, Quincy, Michigan (1990).* By 1995 both Hillsdale and Quincy were listed in the *Michigan Directory* thirty-nine and eighteen years after their founding. However, *The Communicator,* founded in 1999 and published in Allen County, states on its masthead "Reaching over 700 Amish families in Adams, Allen, LaGrange & Whitley Counties, Indiana and Bronson, Camden and Quincy Michigan." The Hillsdale and Quincy Amish share more surnames with Allen County, Indiana, Amish than with Michigan Amish.

The Amish believe that marriage must be "in the Lord," meaning that both partners must be members of the Amish church. This marriage pattern is highly protective of the community and of the family, supporting and reinforcing both institutions. It also perpetuates ethnicity. Divorce is not recognized by the Amish. In the exceedingly rare instances that a member initiates a divorce, the spouse may not remarry as long as the former partner is alive. The individual who initiated the divorce is automatically expelled from the church; the

Figure 7. Amish couple

obedient party retains membership. The whole Amish culture is supportive of marriage. If men and women eat together at a social function, husband and wife are seated next to one another. Marriage is not seen as a romantic journey but as a loving, working partnership for the raising of children and the support of the community.[15] It is expected that there will be difficult times but that with the help of God, the extended family, and the community, the couple will be able to work through these periods and develop a better relationship. Children are a gift from God. God determines when one lives and when one dies; therefore, there are no circumstances when a Christian may kill a human being.

The distribution of last names among the Amish illustrates the degree of social isolation and the pattern of intermarriage. Among the 627 household heads listed in the *1995 Michigan Directory*, sixty-one surnames are found. Fifteen names are represented by only one family, which means that 612 families share forty-six family names. Forty percent of the Michigan Amish have one of four names: Miller, Yoder, Bontrager or Hochstetler/Hostetler. A scribe from Reading, Michigan wrote that among the 72 families in their settlement: "Our group of families are sporting 7 different last names with Schwartz the most common as there are 31 Schwartz families."[16] Homogeneity characterizes Amish communities.

Amish Recipes

CORN COB SYRUP

6 red corn cobs (washed). Boil 1 hour in 3 quart water. Strain, then add 3 lb. Brown sugar and water enough to make 3 quart. Boil until thick enough to suit or to consistency of maple syrup.

Be sure to select clean corn cobs, free from mold. Light colored cobs will make a lighter syrup and give a better flavor.

Favorite Amish Family Recipes (Aylmer, Ont., and LaGrange, Ind.: Pathway Publishing Corp., 1975), 244.

GROUNDCHERRY PIE

2 cups groundcherries	Dash of salt
3 tablespoons flour	1 teaspoon lemon juice
¾–1 cup sugar	Oleo
half-and-half or milk	

Mix sugar, flour, salt and bits of oleo: add to groundcherries and mix. Put in 9-inch unbaked pie crust, then pour on half and half, or just milk to fill the pan. Bake 10 minutes at 400°, then at 325° for 35 to 40 minutes. [Anna Gascho]

(Groundcherries grow on a plant in garden. It reseeds itself and comes up year after year once it's started. Has a very mild taste of its own. [Anna Marie Helmuth])

Oscoda County Amish, Mio, Mich. *Home Cooking.* (Audubon, Iowa: Jumbo Jack Cookbooks, 1994), 177.

Culture Conflicts

The strong emphasis the Amish place on the importance of community is diametrically opposed to the emphasis on individualism prevalent in mainstream American culture. In a population of 170,000 there is bound to be deviant behavior and mental illness. There is an attempt to deal with problem behavior within the family and the community. However, the Amish will use outside professionals when cases of severe mental illness are recognized. Treatment of the individual is often

MAPLE PIE

1 cup maple syrup	⅓ cup melted margarine
4 beaten eggs	1 cup walnuts
½ cup sugar	Dash of salt

Combine and put in unbaked shell. Bake at 350° for 35 minutes. [Mrs. John (Loma) Kauffman]

Oscoda County Amish, Mio, Mich. *Home Cooking* (Audubon, Iowa: Jumbo Jack Cookbooks, 1994), 177.

MENU FOR WEDDINGS AND BARN RAISINGS

65 fryers or 110 lb.	25–30 cakes (15 angel food
hamburger (meatloaf)	15 loaf cakes)
20 gal. potatoes (150 lb.)	26–28 serving bowls pudding
(mashed)	2 (20 qts.) cans coffee
2 (12 qt.) kettles gravy	16 lb. butter (plenty for table
40 lb. frozen peas	and cooking)
26 platters plate salad	6–7 qt. jam
16 gal. fruit	370 dinner buns

Serves approximately 360–370 people. [Sadie Gingerich]

Oscoda County Amish, Mio, Mich. *Home Cooking* (Audubon, Iowa: Jumbo Jack Cookbooks, 1994), 218.

hampered because psychiatrists and many social workers do not understand the strength of the Amish community, both to punish and to support its members. They do not understand the high value placed on obedience, submission, and genuine aid for one another and support for the community as a whole, even at considerable cost to the individual. During the last decade the Amish have developed a peer counseling system that parallels their school system in that it helps both the individual and the community survive in contemporary

Figure 8. Amish boys with "English" visitor. The boys are in everyday clothes, show-ing the beltless, broad-fall trousers and suspenders prescribed by the Ordnung. *The little girl is the author's daughter.*

America. Both systems have well-constructed and continually develop-ing informal methods of training and supervision. Both help the indi-vidual to be an active, functioning member of a close-knit community and to survive in the modern world. The Amish counselors meet together for instruction and discussion. Proceedings of these seminars may be published for use within the larger Amish community.[17] When dealing with serious cases of mental illness, Amish counselors will work with sympathetic "English" mental health professionals. There is one residential community for Amish with emotional problems here in Michigan and another is in the development process. In those cases where emotional or mental illness can be distinguished from stub-bornness or willful disobedience, the Amish community is generally supportive and tolerant of the disturbed individual.

The Amish community is a voluntary community. Individuals may not join it until they are adults, are able to make a mature decision, and are ready to accept the limitations and responsibilities membership requires. Children can misbehave, but they cannot sin as they unable to distinguish right from wrong. Children's behavior is the responsibility of their parents, who teach them how to become mature, God-fearing members of the Amish community. When children graduate from school after completing the eighth grade, the parents relax somewhat their strict supervision of these teenagers. Because the young person has not yet joined church, the community can exert only informal control. This is often a difficult period for the young person (and for his parents) as each individual must personally make what is considered the most important decision of his/her life: whether or not to join church (and generally soon afterwards, whom to marry.) It is a period of relative freedom, of testing the boundaries of their church, sampling what they will reject if they join the community, and experimenting with what they believe to be right or wrong. The degree of rebellion varies from family to family and from community to community but, generally, the individual eventually determines that the lure of "the world" cannot compete with his or her internalized code of ethics. The individual then joins a small group of his/her peers and after a period of teaching the young people are baptized, which washes away their youthful sins and initiates them into the church-community. The recognized and institutionalized few years of individuation act as a safety valve for the individual, the family, and the community, and is a significant and strengthening aspect of the Amish culture.

About 25% of those born into Amish families either do not join the church or leave it at sometime during their adulthood. Those who never join are not participants, but they are neither banned nor shunned. Those who join and then leave are put under the *Bann* and are shunned because they have broken the vow they made at baptism to be a supportive member of the church. Being under the *Bann* can be a very painful experience both for the individual and for his/her family. The *Bann* functions effectively to keep the church strong and homogeneous. In biblical terms it perpetuates a church "without spot or blemish" by removing those who are uncooperative and disobedient.

Figure 9. Teenage girl.

Rejection of aspects of modern technology and tenacious clinging to specific symbols of separation from the larger society, combined with community decision making, have led to misunderstanding and friction between the Amish and the "English." The issues of nonpayment of social security tax, along with refusal to accept social security benefits, were resolved before the main migration to Michigan.[18] The Amish pay property taxes even though they do not send their children to public schools or vote in national elections. They also pay income taxes.

Selective Service has posed a problem for the non-resistant Amish who will not participate in the military but are willing to register as conscientious objectors. The military draft removed young men from the protective community. Most Amish men accepted alternative service but some Amish young men have served prison sentences either because their draft boards judged them insincere or because they would not cooperate fully with Selective Service. At least four Amish men served time in the Federal Prison in Milan, Michigan during the Vietnam War for refusing to accept alternative service, which would have required living in a city and wearing non-Amish clothes while at work.

The Amish refusal to use electricity, refusal to allow milk collection on Sunday and, in some communities, refusal to utilize bulk milk tanks, excludes their milk from the fluid market. Fresh milk in ten-gallon cans is sold to cheesemakers and formerly was sold to companies that produce canned and powdered milk. Michigan Amish who had sold to the Pet milk company for thirty-one years were informed that, even though processing at the plant destroys any bacteria, no milk would be collected that was not cooled to 50° F. In the hot summer weather this cannot be achieved using spring water as the coolant. The Amish who persisted in not using bulk milk tanks cooled by electricity could no longer sell to the milk processing plants.[19] The situation was improved with the building of a new cheese house near Camden, in addition to the one near Six Lakes. There are now four cheese houses in Michigan that enable about three hundred non-electric Amish dairy farmers to continue to produce milk.[20]

Horse-drawn transportation on the roads and highways has, in certain communities, caused a conflict over the use of the orange triangle or slow-moving vehicle sign. Some Amish church districts see these triangles as decorations, ostentatious state symbols, official emblems, symbols of government authority, a type of "graven image," or simply as symbolic of modern times. These Amish feel strongly enough about the symbols to emigrate from areas where they are being ticketed for nondisplay of the slow-moving-vehicle emblem. In the past the Amish have moved from Tennessee to Kentucky, and from Ohio to Michigan, to avoid confrontation. In 1980 three Amish men in Gladwin County were charged with violation of a Michigan statute and local ordinance that required display of a slow-moving vehicle emblem designed by the state. After the case (*The People of Michigan v. Swartzentruber, et al.*) was lost by the Amish at the county level, it went on to the Michigan Court of Appeals. Eight years later the ruling was reversed, holding that the state had failed to prove that Amish buggies, marked by two-inch wide strips of reflective tape roughly outlining the exterior sides of the buggy, presented a safety hazard to the public. As various individuals have commented, "Most drivers don't need to see an emblem to know a horse-drawn buggy isn't going fast." Ohio, Kentucky, and Minnesota now permit the use of reflector tape instead of the slow-moving-vehicle symbol; New York has reached an informal compromise.[21] A lawyer involved in the Michigan slow-moving vehicle case wrote:

> Here again come into focus those elements which have often marked Anabaptist life: *not* waging of polemical warfare, *not* trying to impose their way on others, but instead the mere attempt to live a life in this world according to a certain way given in Scripture. And it is really, then, *the World*, which, unwilling to allow that way to exist, becomes the religious contestant, the wager of ideological wars, the imposer of its values.[22]

Education

The conflict of values between the Amish and the state is raised dramatically in the area of education. The Amish do not believe that children belong to the state, but to God. They believe that parents are accountable to God for their children who are a gift from Him. Therefore, certain aspects of education are not negotiable. If the state intrudes beyond a certain point, the Amish will move away. Forcing Amish children to attend high school helped push the Amish in Jerome to leave Michigan. All the Amish moved out of the state of Nebraska when denied their own schools and their own teachers. (Nebraska laws were liberalized, but the Amish had already left.) There is a long history of conflict between the Amish and the Michigan Board of Education.

Legislative regulation of nonpublic schools is used to: (1) reinforce school attendance requirements, (2) prevent teaching of socially dangerous ideas, (3) promote cultural unity and (4) to protect the public from dangerous business, health, and building practices.[23] Each of these areas is open to different interpretations by the Amish and the State Board of Education. In Michigan the superintendent of public instruction is granted supervision of all private, denominational, and parochial schools in the state and is thereby responsible for "the sanitary conditions of such schools, the course of study therein and the qualifications of the teachers thereof shall be of the same standard as provided by the general school laws of the state."[24] In order to be qualified, Michigan law requires that all nonpublic school teachers be certified (only five other states have this requirement). For the course of study to be of the same standard, the nonpublic schools must teach courses comparable to those taught in the public schools. If all the requirements of the Michigan Educational Act are not met by a school, the pupils are considered to be in violation of the state attendance requirements. The children can be declared truant, the parents arrested, and the school closed.

Michigan Amish schools are housed either in old one-room public schoolhouses or in buildings erected to specifications approved by the state.[25] The school building usually consists of a single room, heated by a woodburning stove. There is no electricity or indoor plumbing nor is there likely to be a basement. Children study by natural light from windows and use outhouses; water is provided by a single faucet or pump.[26] School rooms are pleasant and uncluttered, with desks arranged in straight rows facing the teacher and the blackboard. A bulletin board, posters displaying the name and grade of each child, some mottoes, and perhaps drawings done by the pupils or teacher are the only decorations. Typically one teacher supervises all eight grades; however, about a third of the Michigan Amish schools have two teachers for the eight grades. The average number of pupils per teacher is about fifteen. The Michigan Amish prefer to establish a new school for additional pupils rather than enlarge an existing school.[27] All instruction is in English except for German class, which may be held once a week for the older children, generally taught by a male volunteer from the community. Some of the textbooks are reprintings of older public school texts. Many, especially English readers and history texts, are written by Amish men and women and produced by Amish publishers or printers. Religion is not part of the curriculum, for religious training is the responsibility of the parents, rather than the school or even the church.[28] At school each morning a short selection from the Bible is read and one or two hymns sung—all without discussion.

Figure 10. Michigan schoolhouse, with bell, outhouses, play equipment, and buggies.

Children are given a realistic appraisal of their abilities. Although hard work and efficient use of time are valued more than academic brilliance, grades are based solely on mastery of subject matter. Children are graded by absolute standards, not in comparison with one another. Competition is minimized with cooperation and individual responsibility being emphasized. The Golden Rule, do unto others as you would have others do unto you, is taught as the basis for personal interaction. Two Michigan Amish schools are named Golden Rule School. Children in Amish schools, taught by teachers trained in Amish schools, performed as well as their non-Amish peers on the Iowa Test of Basic skills.[29] Careful records of attendance are kept and submitted promptly to the state. Unlike charter schools no money is accepted from the state.

Although Amish teachers have a formal education only through the eighth grade, many take correspondence courses and receive practical instruction from fellow teachers and the *Blackboard Bulletin*.[30] Local and regional teachers' meetings and visits to other schools also function as in-service training. Amish teachers are selected because of their ability to work with children, parents, and members of the Amish community. They must be good role models, able to maintain discipline, and have themselves been good students. New teachers receive

Figure 11. Self-portrait by ten-year-old Amish schoolgirl.

varying amounts of formal training, often working as teacher's helpers before having their own school. Amish teachers are more concerned with giving their students correct knowledge than with critical thinking. The primary method used to instill facts is memorization and drill. Teachers do not consider themselves to be ultimate authorities, and they are willing to admit to the parents and to the children that they make mistakes. Character (moral) development is considered as important as intellectual development.

The first Amish school in Michigan was opened in 1958 near Camden by Amish settlers who, two years earlier, had moved from Indiana hoping to avoid confrontations with school authorities. A second school in the same Hillsdale County settlement opened in 1960. The Amish in Branch County opened a third school in 1962. Trouble began in 1963 when eleven Hillsdale Amish fathers were served warrants. Local opinion and the general citizenry supported the Amish but the superintendent of public instruction was determined to prosecute and kept pressure on the local authorities to bring the Amish fathers to trial. In 1965 ten Amish families sold their farms and moved to regions of Indiana and Ohio where they could operate their own schools. As a result of this exodus, one Hillsdale Amish school closed for lack of pupils. Joel Schwartz, the father of ten children, whose 166-acre farm was auctioned off at a loss of about $25 per acre, said:

Indiana welcomed us.

I hated to go. Of any place I ever lived it hurt the most to leave Camden. I liked the community and I liked the people. They were good to us and easy to get along with.[31]

The controversy continued with attempts at legal solutions and reinterpretations of state educational procedures. Feelings ran high. While the Michigan Education Association, some legislators and various liberal organizations took a strong stand against permitting Amish schools to operate, most of the general population tolerated or even supported the Amish position. In 1966, after three years and some changes in personnel, Michigan's State Board of Education approved a plan that would permit the Camden Amish to continue operating their school "for at least one year." Under this plan the superintendent of the county's intermediate school district was legally the "teacher" or curriculum supervisor. In this capacity the supervisor visited each Amish school four times a year, observed the Amish "teacher's aides" instructing their pupils, and filed a report with the state Department of Education.[32] In 1993, after visiting a school, one of the state officials reassured the Amish present that as long as they could achieve the academic level she had observed that day there would be no cause to force them to have certified teachers.[33] The Amish have no real guarantee that they may continue to operate their schools in Michigan. The State Board of Education periodically threatens to close them.[34] So far the Amish schools, supported by public opinion, have remained open and Amish continue to establish communities in rural Michigan.

In spite of the many problems, the expense involved and the great

Table 4: Michigan Amish Schools

DIRECTORY DATE	NUMBER OF SCHOOLS*	NUMBER OF TEACHERS	NUMBER OF PUPILS
1970	3	3	63
1975	10	10	183
1980	14	15	373
1985	19	24	425
1990	32	33	776
1995	55	67	1,253
2000	66	89	1,362

* Reporting by schools is incomplete so these figures are estimates.

Souces: "Teachers' Directory 1970," *Blackboard Bulletin,* Nov. 1970, 98; "School Directory 1975–76," *Blackboard Bulletin,* Jan. 1976, 12; "School Directory 1980–81," *Blackboard Bulletin,* Nov. 1980, 12–13; "School Directory 1985–86," *Blackboard Bulletin,* Nov. 1985, 13–14; "School Directory 1990–91," *Blackboard Bulletin,* Jan. 1991, 10–11; "School Directory 1995–96," *Blackboard Bulletin,* Nov. 1995, 12–13, 28; "School Directory 1999–00," *Blackboard Bulletin,* Nov. 1999, 10–11.

effort required, the number of Amish schools has increased in direct proportion to the increase in Amish population in the state. An Amish-run school has become as important for new community survival as an organized church district. Amish rarely home-school, as they believe children need to learn to work and play together and must learn to take their place in the community. Today new settlements organize a school for their children as soon as the first families arrive. In 1970 there were only three Amish schools in Michigan; twenty years later there were thirty-six; by 2000 there were sixty-six. The number of Amish children attending these schools has increased from 63 to about 1,400.

Medicine

In addition to having no state-certified teachers, the Amish have no licensed medical doctors. Contrary to popular belief, the Amish generally

Amish Cures

INSECT-REPELLING FORMULA FOR VEGETABLE CROPS

5 pounds white sugar

1 quart Bo-Peep Ammonia

1 pint 35% hydrogen peroxide

1 gallon vinegar without additives (We prefer our own homemade vinegar.)

100 milligrams Vitamin B-12 liquid

Combine and mix with 20 gallons of water

Sprays one acre. This has worked for us for 5 years, sometimes it works very well, other times it doesn't. We have used it for many different insects.

Raymond J. Yoder, *Growing Produce Family Style* (n.p., 1996), 75.

POISON IVY

Wash off with sassafras, jewel weed, or a broom sage tea.

Rub the inside of a banana skin on the affected parts. It is also recommended to rub the inside of a still juicy lemon or orange peel over the poison.

Take a sprig of oak bark about 2" × 4", boil in 1 quart of water for 5 minutes, then simmer for 1 hour. Apply to affected area often. This will relieve the itching also.

Grandma's Home Remedies (n.p., 1991), 44–45.

CLOVER BLOSSOM SALVE

Take pound for pound of clover blossoms and vaseline (petroleum jell). Heat in a very slow oven or in the hot sun for an hour. Strain through a thin cloth and

make use of and cooperate fully with members of the medical profession, both in treatment and research. They also make use of alternative and natural or folk medicine. Both types of treatment may be used simultaneously. Very modern medical practices may be mentioned in the same *Budget* column as a simple home remedy. There are Amish individuals who are interested in and knowledgeable about healing practices. These individuals may run health food stores and help with health problems. They do not charge for their services, though they store in jars. This works wonders for chapped hands and for cows' chapped teats.

Grandma's Home Remedies (n.p., 1991), 52.

INSOMNIA

Soak your feet in bearably hot water in which a small amount of vinegar has been added, just before retiring. (Instead of soaking the feet, they can be rubbed well with a warm vinegar/water solution to induce sleep.)

Grandma's Home Remedies (n.p., 1991), 35.

BRONSON, MICHIGAN

Jan. 4—Esther Stutzman had to have a few stitches put in her head but she's getting along as good as can be expected. Clara, dau. of Edward Schmuckers., had gall trouble Sat. night and was in the emergency room for awhile. She came home again. Jacob Brandenberger, (Sonny) will have a prostate gland operation.

Jan. 3rd church service was held at Joni R. Hershbergers'. Strangers were Daniel Millers from Ind, Joe Schwartzes and son, Monroe Nisleys from Iowa, and Pre. Mervin Millers from Centreville, Mich. Church will be held at Levi Stutzmans' Jan. 17th.

Our community has 9 families, 19 scholars, one widow, one school; and 25 young folks. Anna Hershberger teach ½ turn and Frieda Schmucker ½ turn. Two babies were born in 1992 and we had one wedding.

—Kathryn Hershberger, *Budget,* 13 January 1993

may accept donations. An example of an alternative practice is using a dressing of clean plantain, burdock, or grape leaves that have been soaked briefly in hot (180°F) water. The leaves are placed over a burn, under a gauze bandage. The bandage is changed twice a day with little pain as the leaves keep the surface of the burn moist and prevent painful sticking of the bandage to the burned flesh.[35] Some remedies are more problematic. "Painkiller: Take powdered poke root roasted ¼ cup. Add enough water to make a poultice and apply on bottom of feet.

It will draw out pain anywhere in the body."[36] "Cold sores: Drink sage tea. Hold the tea in your mouth before swallowing."[37]

In cases of serious illness, Amish will go to the University of Michigan Hospital from all over the state and from Indiana and occasionally Canada. They also go to local Michigan hospitals and, in complicated cases, to Mayo Clinic. Amish patients are transported by ambulance and even by helicopter. The critically ill Amish patient accepts the most modern technology. Amish have had heart, kidney, and bone marrow transplants. They accept blood transfusions and treatment with pressurized oxygen, radiation, and chemotherapy if they perceive the treatments as necessary to restore health.[38] The most sophisticated life support systems are tolerated, at least briefly. The Amish do not fear death; it is God's will for each of us and should not be needlessly postponed. When an eighteen-year-old boy in Pennsylvania received severe head injuries, he was rushed to the nearest hospital and placed on a respirator. Two days later (Friday), the attending doctors pronounced him brain dead and it was decided to remove him from the machine.

> Another health official stepped in before he was released and refused to release his body. This caused undue agony to the already bereaved family. His body could not be released from the machine, while the official claimed he was still breathing, until Monday. . . . You will note that the obituary in the *Lancaster News*, says that he died on Monday. The time of death and age were announced at the funeral as on [Friday].[39]

The Amish community did not consider a body kept alive by a machine to still be a living person, "the truth was that his soul had fled."[40]

The dying person is not necessarily the unfortunate one. The day before his death, I was sitting in the hospital room with a middle-aged Amish man and his wife, waiting for the arrival of his children. The husband was restless and though not in pain was uncomfortable. His wife said to him, almost sharply, "It's easier for you, you'll be in heaven soon and I'll be left here all alone." Though the survivors have the more difficult role, they can take comfort in the belief that their loved one is in heaven and the separation is only temporary.

Sometimes the medical establishment does not understand that it may be perceived as better for a person to die sooner, surrounded by the soothing love and nurture of family, than to live a few weeks, months, or even several years longer, enduring physical and emotional pain.[41] Doctors may not understand that a good death is preferable to postponing death. A respected Amish minister was placed on a respirator following an operation at the University of Michigan. The patient, his wife, and his ten children, all of whom were present, wanted him removed from the respirator so he could council them before he died, but the hospital refused. "We never, ever consider removing a patient while he is still conscious. He will live at the most a few days if we take him off." Instead he lived just ten more days and now, many years later, his family and his church are still suffering from lack of closure. The surgeon could not comprehend that it was more important to have settled the things of this world than it was to remain in the world.

Cultural Persistance

The Amish are often perceived as rigid and unchanging, as fossilized peasants or, more charitably, as everyone's great-grandparents. However, in order to survive the strains and stresses of the fast changing society in which they are immersed, the Amish must be able to adapt. Paradoxically, the Amish change in order not to change. Under specific circumstances they are willing to modify their behavior in order to remain steadfast to their values. An Amish leader succinctly expressed the difference between modifying behavior and modifying values. The title of an editorial in the *Blackboard Bulletin* expressed this difference concisely, "Co-operate? Most Certainly! Compromise? Never!" The author continued, "There is a world of difference between refusing to co-operate on matters of no religious significance, and refusing to compromise in our religious beliefs."[42] This willingness to change behavior in order to preserve values is vividly demonstrated by development of an Amish school system. An Amish school is now almost as important as resident clergy for community success. Additionally the Amish are developing their own counseling system and are helping to establish cheesehouses to use the milk that they

Figure 12. Amish dolls on Amish-made porch glider. Amish dolls are faceless to avoid even a suspicion of a "graven image."

cannot otherwise sell; they help build and staff rural birthing centers and clinics; and they are establishing produce cooperatives and auctions. Though the Amish remain strictly congregational they have formalized a nation-wide steering committee that meets to discuss and evaluate relations with the civil government. Many church districts have a semi-formal plan to help with hospital expenses and disasters such as tornadoes, fires, or other accidents. This sharing of extraordinary expenses protects the land base of the community because families are not forced to sell off acreage in order to meet catastrophic expenses. This sharing of education and helping in time of need are modern extensions of "bearing one another's burdens." And, by sharing one another's burdens they are able to maintain their cultural identity.

The Amish increasingly contribute to Michigan's diversity, adding to the rich texture of cultures. They impose few demands on the state, asking only to be left alone to follow their distinctive road to eternal life. The Michigan Amish do not burden social services with abused children, battered wives, or drug-addicted individuals. They have no homeless members, no abandoned babies, and only short-term residents in nursing homes. They do not clog the legal system and rarely populate our jails. Usually, they can care for their own problem individuals within their own communities. Yet, though the Amish do not burden society neither do they produce astronauts, stockbrokers, ballet dancers, or neurosurgeons. Instead they are a hard-working, frugal, family-centered people who in many ways exemplify values and a way of life characteristic of an earlier time—an era when people were in touch with the land, with the flow of nature, with the workings of their own neighborhood. The Amish method of farming does not produce a large cash flow but functions to preserve communities and the land, and is ecologically and psychologically sound. By limiting technology, the Amish remind a restless and materialistic society that there are advantages to austerity and simplicity. By preventing sensory overload, they free themselves to enjoy physical work, the natural world, and the shared traditions of their culture. As our lives become ever more complicated and our roles more specialized, perhaps we may learn something from a people who do not freely embrace technology nor automatically embrace progress, who attempt to control technology in order that it may not control them. By allowing the Amish the freedom to reject our values we protect our own values and our own freedom.

Notes

1. I wish to thank David Luthy for making available the resources of the Heritage Historical Library, Aylmer, Ontario and for his personal help and consultation.
2. *The Budget,* 11 November 1981.
3. The historical material is from consultation with Amish historians, Joseph Stoll and David Luthy, and from John A. Hostetler, *Amish Society,* 4th ed. (Baltimore: Johns Hopkins University Press) 1993, the definitive book on the Amish.
4. David Luthy, *The Amish in America: Settlements that Failed, 1840–1960,* (Aylmer, Ontario: Pathway Publishers, 1986), 196. The information on extinct settlements is primarily from this source and from personal communication with David Luthy.
5. In 1954 the bishop died and the ministers had already moved away. Seven women who were either single or widows were the only remaining Old Order Amish. A minister from Indiana had oversight for a time. When Amish settlers moved in from Ohio, these women joined the new church and accepted its *Ordnung.*
6. The Swiss Amish speak a Swiss German dialect rather than the Palatinate German dialect of the typical Pennsylvania Dutch. They also still sing nineteenth-century Swiss yodeling songs.

7. Luthy, *Settlements*, 204.

8. *Shagbark Hickory* (1981) and *Michigan Summer* (1998) by Joseph Stoll describe Amish boyhood in Jerome.

9. "English" is a term used to describe any person, thing, or activity that is not Amish.

10. *Budget*, 12 June 1991.

11. DeVon Miller, *Michigan Directory 1995* (Millersburg, Ohio: Albana Book Service, 1995.)

12. Of the twenty-seven settlements in Michigan in 1995, nineteen are included in the *Directory*. Some church districts in the included settlements did not report. Some individual families were not included. The data are nevertheless fairly representative, although slightly skewed toward assimilation and away from the most conservative churches.

13. Charlotte, Mich., 22 January 1997.

14. Gertrude Enders Huntington, "Occupational Opportunities for Old Order Amish Women," *Pennsylvania Folklore* (Spring 1994): 115–20.

15. Huntington, "The Amish Family," in *Ethnic Families in America: Patterns and Variations*, 3d ed., ed. Charles H. Mindel, Robert W. Habenstein, and Roosevelt Wright Jr. (New York: Elsevier Science Publishing Co., 1988), 367–99.

16. *Budget*, 12 January 2000.

17. Family Helpers, *Marriage Meeting* (n.p., 1997).

18. Amish working in factories or for outsiders must pay social security taxes, but self-employed Amish or those working for other Amish need not pay. Amish do not accept social security benefits and reject Medicare and Medicaid.

19. *Budget*, 5, 12, 19 June and 10, July 1991.

20. In 1992 there was concern that the 50° F temperature requirements would be applied to grade B milk. Senator Jack Welborn called a meeting of Amish leaders and dairy farmers to meet with Department of Agriculture representatives and other state representatives. Although the Amish generally do not vote they are willing to meet with legislators to explain their positions and beliefs. Public Act 134, passed in 1993 enabled the Amish to continue to supply milk to the cheese houses.

21. Lee J. Zook, "Slow Moving Vehicles," in *The Amish and the State*, ed. Donald B. Kraybill (Baltimore, Md.: Johns Hopkins University Press, 1993), 145–60.

22. William B. Ball, "An External Perspective: The Constitutional Freedom to Be Anabaptist," *Brethren Life and Thought* 33, no. 3 (1988): 200.

23. John Elson, "State Regulation of Nonpublic Schools: The Legal Framework," In *Public Controls for Nonpublic Schools,* ed. Donald Erickson (Chicago: Universiy of Chicago Press, 1969), 104.

24. Elson, *State Regulation,* 124.

25. A meeting requested by Henry J. Miller, who represented the Amish schools, led to the approval of a basic plan for Amish school buildings (Memorandum from Senator Jack Welborn, 1981, to Henry Miller, Mr. Turnbull, Department of Education and State Fire Marshal.)

26. Due to the expense of frequent water tests mandated by the Environmental Protection Act, in some schools the children bring their own drinking water or water is obtained from two sources, generally neighboring farms.

27. "Before one-room schoolhouses completely disappear," says Scott Westerman, dean of the School of Education at Eastern Michigan University, "We are taking steps to inventory them to determine their current number, use, and condition. In the process, we hope to draw citizen attention to this practical and symbolic edifice of our American educational system." Further along in the article, Thomas L. Jones, executive director of the Historical Society of Michigan, is quoted at saying, "To us, the one-room schoolhouse harkens back to the days of dedicated teachers, along with their students, covering the educational basics and, in the process, educating the child of rural America ("One-Room Schoolhouse Survey" 1991.)

28. Huntington, "Persistence and Change in Amish Education," in *The Amish Struggle With Modernity,* ed. Donald B. Kraybill and Marc A. Olshan (Hanover and London: University Press of New England, 1994), 77–95.

29. John Hostetler and Gertrude Enders Huntington, *Amish Children: Education in the Family, School and Community,* 2d ed. (Fort Worth, Texas: Harcourt, Brace, Jovanovich, College Publishers, 1992).

30. The *Blackboard Bulletin* is a monthly periodical published since 1957 in the interest of Old Order Amish and Old Order Mennonite schools by an Amish publishing house, Pathway Publishers, Alymer, Ontario. It contains practical suggestions on all aspects of teaching, case studies, discussion of problems and inspirational articles for teachers.

31. Page 230 of Wayne L. Fischer's manuscript; edited quotation on page 120 of Wayne L. Fisher, *The Amish in Court* (New York: AMS Press, 1993).

32. Robert Holden, "The Amish Among Us," *Ann Arbor News*, 17 June 1970; W. Fisher, *Court*, 111–27.

33. The exchange was described to me as follows: "The law in Michigan is that all private or parochial schools must have certified teachers, but in 1993 the superintendent of public instruction visited our school and after observing the children studying and examining their work and the teacher's methods and the school records, she was asked,

> "Do you see anytime in the future that the state will force us to have certified teachers?" After a pause she said,
> "No." I asked,
> "How can you as a state official say 'no' when the law states 'yes?'" She answered.
> "What I have observed here today—you are fulfilling the spirit of the law without the law and we cannot do that with the law." I asked,
> "Why can't you?"
> "We don't have the building blocks you have."
> "What are those?"
> "You have family, church, and school and the great part of the public children don't have a close family life or attend church, we only have a school . . . As long as you can achieve the academic level I have observed here today we have no cause to force you to have certified teachers."
> —*Henry J. Miller, personal communication.*

34. Lisa Zagaroli, "Amish Fear for Schools," *Ann Arbor News*, 4 July 1990.

35. John W. Keim, *Comfort for the Burned and Wounded* (Quakertown, Penn.: The Philosophical Publishing Company, 1999), 27–41.

36. Wickey Sisters, *Amish Home Remedies* (Gordonville, Penn. print shop, 1991), 46.

37. [Sarah Weaver], *Over One Hundred of Grandma's Home Remedies: The Plain People's Method on How to Cut Down on Doctor Bills* (n. p. 1988), 18.

38. Huntington, "Cultural Interaction During Time of Crisis: Boundary Maintenance and Amish Boundary Definition." In *Internal and External Perspectives of Amish and Mennonite Life*, ed. Werner Enninger (Essen, Germany: Unipress, 1984), 92–118; Huntington, "Health Care," in *Amish and the State*, ed. Donald B. Kraybill (Baltimore, Md.: Johns Hopkins University Press, 1993), 163–89.

39. "Community Notes," *The Diary* (December 1979): 2.

40. Memorial poem, *Budget*, 1980.

41. Ronald C. Drake, "A Deadly Illness: A Choice for Amish," *Philadelphia Inquirer,* 24 February 1991; Roland and Mary Weiler, "To Love and to Lose," *Family Life* (June 1991): 15–17; Huntington, "Health Care," 163–89.

42. *Blackboard Bulletin* (February 1960); Joseph Stoll, "Co-operate? Most Certainly! Compromise? Never!" in *Challenge of the Child* (Aylmer, Ont.: Pathway Publishers, 1975), 120–22.

For Further Reference

Printed Sources

Amish Directory: Allen County, South Whitley, Quincy, Michigan. N.p. , December 1990.

Ball, William B. "An External Perspective: The Constitutional Freedom to Be Anabaptist." *Brethren Life and Thought* 33, no. 3 (1988): 200–4.

Beechy, William, and Malinda Beechy, eds. *Experiences of C.O.'s in C. P. S. Camps in 1-W Service in Hospitals, and During World War I.* LaGrange, Indiana: n.d.

Biggs, Mark. "Conservation Farmland Management: The Amish Family Farm versus Modern Corn Belt Agriculture." Master's thesis, Pennsylvania State University, 1981.

"The Bill of Rights and the Amish." *The People Speak* 1, no. 4. Grand Rapids, Michigan. Includes articles by Russell Kirk, an interview with George W. Walsh, and "An Open Letter to Governor Romney." 1966.

Blackboard Bulletin. Monthly periodical published in the interest of Old Order Amish and Old Order Mennonite schools: Aylmer, Ont.: Pathway Publishers, 1957–.

Brandenburger, Enos. *Indiana Amish Directory: Allen County and Vicinity, including Dekalb and Steuben Counties in Indiana and Hillsdale County in Michigan.* N.p., 1970.

The Budget. A weekly newspaper serving Sugarcreek, Ohio and Amish and Mennonite communities.1981, 11 November; 1990, 17 January; 1991, 5,12, 19, June, 10 July; 13 January 1993; 1997, 22 January; 2000, 12 January, 1890–.

Byler, Uria. *School Bells Ringing: A Manual for Amish Teachers and Parents.* Aylmer, Ont. and LaGrange, Ind.: Pathway Publishers, 1969.

"Community Notes." *The Diary.* Gordonville, Pennsylvania: Pequea Publishers (December 1979): 2.

The Diary. A monthly periodical devoted to Amish history and genealogy. Gordonville, Penn.: Pequea Publishers, 1969–.

Drake, Ronald C. "A Deadly Illness: A Choice for Amish." *Philadelphia Inquirer,* 24 February 1991.

Elson, John. "State Regulation of Nonpublic Schools: The Legal Framework." In *Public Controls for Nonpublic Schools,* Edited by Donald Erickson. Chicago: University of Chicago Press, 1969.

Family Life. Monthly publication dedicated to promoting Christian living among plain people. Aylmer, Ontario: Pathway Publishers. Complete years available on microfilm from Bell & Howell Information and Learning, Ann Arbor, Michigan. 1968–.

Fisher, Gideon L. *Farm Life and Its Changes.* Gordonville, Penn.: Pequea Publishers, 1978.

Fisher, Wayne L. *The Amish in Court.* New York: AMS Press, 1993.

Holden, Robert. "The Amish Among Us." *Ann Arbor News,* 17 June 1970.

Hostetler, John A. *Amish Society.* 4th ed. Baltimore and London: Johns Hopkins Press, 1993.

———. ed. *Amish Roots: A Treasury of History, Wisdom and Lore.* Baltimore and London: Johns Hopkins University Press, 1989.

Hostetler, John A., and Gertrude Enders Huntington. *Amish Children: Education in the Family, School and Community.* 2d ed. Case Studies in Cultural Anthropology, Edited by George and Louise Spindler. Fort Worth, Texas: Harcourt, Brace, Jovanovich, College Publishers, 1992.

Howard-Filler, Saralee R. "Michigan's Plain People." *Michigan History* 66, no. 3 (1982): 24–33.

Huntington, Gertrude Enders. "Cultural Interaction During Time of Crisis: Boundary Maintenance and Amish Boundary Definition." In *Internal and External Perspectives of Amish and Mennonite Life.* Edited by Werner Enninger. Essen, Germany: Unipress, 1984.

————. "The Amish Family." In *Ethnic Families in America: Patterns and Variations*, 3d ed. Edited by Charles H. Mindel, Robert W, Habenstein, and Roosevelt Wright Jr. New York: Elsevier Science Publishing Co., 1988.

————. "Health Care." In *Amish and the State*. Edited by Donald B. Kraybill. Baltimore and London: Johns Hopkins University Press, 1993.

————. "Occupational Opportunities for Old Order Amish Women." *Pennsylvania Folklore* (Spring 1994): 115–20.

————. "Persistence and Change in Amish Education." In *The Amish Struggle With Modernity*. Edited by Donald B. Kraybill and Marc A. Olshan. Hanover and London: University Press of New England, 1994.

————. "Amish." In *American Immigrant Cultures: Builders of a Nation*. Vol. 1. Edited by David Levinson and Melvin Ember. New York: Macmillan Reference USA, Simon & Schuster Macmillan, 1997.

Igou, Brad. *The Amish In Their Own Words: Amish Writing From 25 years of "Family Life" Magazine*. Scottdale, Penn., and Waterloo, Ont.: Herald Press, 1999.

Keim, John W. *Comfort for the Burned and Wounded*. Quakertown, Penn.: The Philosophical Publishing Company, 1999.

Kline, David. *Great Possessions: An Amish Farmer's Journal*. San Francisco: North Point Press, 1990.

Kraybill, Donald B. *The Riddle of Amish Culture*. Baltimore and London: Johns Hopkins University Press, 1989.

————, ed. *The Amish and the State*. Baltimore and London: Johns Hopkins University Press, 1993.

Kraybill, Donald, and Marc A. Olshan, eds. *The Amish Struggle with Modernity*. Hanover and London: University Press of New England, 1994.

Longcore, Kathleen. "Amish Among Us." *Grand Rapids (Mich.) Press*, 27 November, 1996.

Luthy, David. Personal communication, 1966–.

————. "A History of *The Budget*." *Family Life* (June and July, 1978): 19–22, 15–18.

————. "History of Raber's Bookstore." *Mennonite Quarterly Review* (April, 1984): 168–78.

————. *Amish Settlements Across America*. Alymer, Ont.: Pathway Publishers, 1985.

————. *The Amish in America: Settlements that Failed 1840–1960*. Aylmer, Ont., and LaGrange, Ind.: Pathway Publishers, 1986.

————. "Amish Settlements Across America: 1991." *Family Life* (April, 1992): 19–34.

————. "Amish Migration Patterns." In *The Amish Struggle with Modernity.* Edited by Donald B. Kraybill and Marc A. Olshan. Hanover and London: University Press of New England, 1994.

————. "Amish Settlements Across America: 1996. *Family Life* (April, 1997): 20–24.

————. *Why Some Amish Communities Fail: Extinct Settlements, 1961–1999.* Aylmer, Ont., and LaGrange, Ind.: Pathway Publishers, 2000.

Miller, DeVon. *Michigan Amish Directory.* N.p., 1987.

————. *Michigan Amish Directory 1995.* Millersburg, Ohio: Albana Book Service, 1995.

Miller, Henry J. *Michigan Amish Directory.* N.p., 1975.

Myers, Thomas J. "Stress and the Amish Community in Transition." Ph.D. diss., Boston University, 1983.

Nolt, Steven M. *A History of the Amish.* Intercourse, Penn.: Good Books, 1999.

"One-Room Schoolhouse Survey." *Historical Society of Michigan Newsletter.* Ann Arbor 14 (1991): 1, 2.

Oscoda County Amish, Mio, Mich. *Home Cooking.* Audubon, Ia.: Jumbo Jack Cookbooks, 1994.

Raber. Ben J. *Der Neue Americanische Calender* and *The New American Almanac.* Yearly publication serving the Amish and Mennonite communities. Baltic, Ohio, 1969–.

Raber, J. A. *Der Neue Amerikanische Calender.* Yearly publication serving the Amish and Mennonite communities. Baltic, Ohio, 1939–68.

Rechlin, A. T. M. 1976. *Spatial Behavior of the Old Order Amish, Nappanee, Indiana.* Michigan Geographical Publication 18. Ann Arbor: University of Michigan Department of Geography.

Stoll, Elmo, and Mark Stoll. *Pioneer Catalogue of County Living.* Toronto: Personal Library Publishers, 1980.

Stoll, Joseph. "Co-operate? Most Certainly! Compromise? Never!" In *Challenge of the Child.* Alymer, Ont.: Pathway Publishers, 1967.

————. "Who Shall Educate Our Children?" In *Compulsory Education and the Amish: The Right Not to Be Modern.* Edited by A. N. Keim. Boston: Beacon Press, 1975.

———. *Shagbark Hickory.* Aylmer, Ont., and LaGrange, Ind.: Pathway Publishers, 1981.

———. *Michigan Summer.* Aylmer, Ont., and LaGrange, Ind.: Pathway Publishers, 1998.

[Stoll, Joseph, et al.?] *1001 Questions and Answers on the Christian Life.* Aylmer, Ont., and LaGrange, Ind.: Pathway Publishers, 1992.

[Weaver, Sarah]. *Over One Hundred of Grandma's Home Remedies: The Plain Peoples' Method on How to Cut Down on Doctor Bill.* N.p., 1988.

Wagler, David. *Keys to Better Health.* Aylmer, Ont., and LaGrange, Ind.: Pathway Publishers, 1998.

Weiler, Roland, and Mary Weiler, "To Love and to Lose." *Family Life* (June 1991): 15–17.

Wickey Sisters, *Amish Home Remedies.* N.p., 1991.

Yoder, Paton, and Steven R. Estes. *Proceedings of the Amish Ministers' Meetings: 1862–1878,* Goshen, Ind.: Indiana Mennonite Historical Society, 1999.

Yoder's Amish Auction,Clare, Mich.. One Friday, May and September.

Yoder, Raymond J., *Growing Produce Family Style.* N.p., 1996.

Zagaroli, Lisa. "Amish Fear For Their Schools." *Ann Arbor News,* 4 July 1990.

Zook, Lee J. "Slow Moving Vehicles." In *The Amish and the State.* Edited by Donald B. Kraybill. Baltimore and London: Johns Hopkins University Press, 1993.

Archives

Michigan State University Library, Michigan State University, East Lansing, MI 48823; (517) 355-2370. Hours: 8–5, Monday–Friday. Material culture holdings include Amish articles. The archival collection has fieldwork notes pertaining to the Amish.

Mennonite Historical Library, Goshen College, 7100 South Main Street, Goshen, IN 46526; (219) 535-7418; E-mail: *mhl@goshen.edu.* Hours: 8–5, Monday–Friday. Extensive collections of material on the Amish.

Heritage Historical Library, Route 4, Aylmer, Ontario, N5H 2R3, Canada. Amish-owned library. Most editions of books used by the Amish Anabaptists since 1525. Extensive collection of twentieth-century Amish ephemera. Write for information on hours and to arrange for visiting.

Museum

Menno-Hof, Shipshewana, IN; (219) 768-4117. Hours: 10–5, Monday–Saturday
(seasonal variation). Museum of history and beliefs of the Mennonites,
Amish and Hutterites

Elderhostel

Amigo Centre, 26455 Banker Road, Sturgis, MI 49091 (Six miles north of Sturgis);
(616) 651-2811. Amish-Mennonite Heritage Course, given twice a year,
includes fieldtrips to visit Amish school, dinner in Amish home, meeting
with church leaders, visit to information center, etc.

Auction

Yoder's Amish Auction, Clare, MI. One Friday in May and in September

Video Resources

The Amish: Not to be Modern. Filmmakers Library, 133 East 58th Street, New York,
NY 10022. Ohio Amish; much of the narration is by Amish individuals.

A People of Preservation. Heritage Productions, 1191 Sumneytown Pike, Harleys-
ville, PA 19438. Amish general information, photographed in Pennsylvania,
narrated by former Amish and knowledgeable scholars.

ACKNOWLEDGMENTS

My deepest thanks to the many members of the Amish faith, who tolerated and educated me as I moved from book learning to real learning.

To John A. Hostetler, with whom I have had the privilege to work for most of my professional life.

To the Joe M. Beachy family, who took me in, and to their children, grandchildren, and great-grandchildren.

To David and Mary Luthy and their children, for many shared scholarly and personal insights and for an affection that continues to grow.

To Arthur W. Helweg, who got me started on this project and who had the imagination and the tenacity to document the many different peoples who create Michigan.

I would like to thank those who read a draft of the text, Henry J. Miller, Wayne Helmuth, Anna Marie Helmuth, David Luthy, and Karen Yoder. They did not see the final manuscript and have no responsibility for its form or content.

I thank the many Amish friends and Anabaptist scholars who have enriched my life.

Index